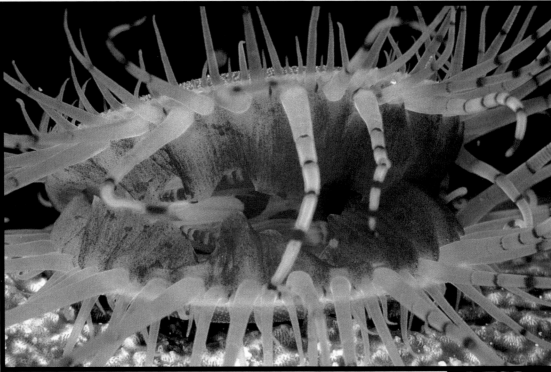

Published by Creative Education
P.O. Box 227, Mankato, Minnesota 56002
Creative Education is an imprint of The Creative Company

Design by Stephanie Blumenthal; Production by The Design Lab
Printed in the United States of America

Photographs by Georgienne Bradley and Jay Ireland
Copyright © 2008 Creative Education
International copyright reserved in all countries. No part of this book may be reproduced in any form
without written permission from the publisher.

Library of Congress Cataloging-in-Publication Data
Frisch, Aaron.
Coral reefs / by Aaron Frisch.
p. cm. — (Our world)
Includes index.
ISBN 978-1-58341-570-2
1. Coral reef ecology—Juvenile literature. 2. Coral reefs and islands—Juvenile literature. I. Title
QH541.5.C7F76 2008    577.7'89—dc22    2006102987

First edition
2 4 6 8 9 7 5 3 1

OUR WORLD

CORAL REEFS

Aaron Frisch

Coral reefs are hard **structures** in the ocean. Coral reefs can be very big. The biggest coral reef is called the Great Barrier Reef. It is by Australia. It is 1,250 miles (2,010 km) long!

Coral reefs are made by little ocean animals called coral polyps *(POLL-ups)*. Polyps usually live in water close to land. They like water that is **shallow** and warm. Coral polyps grow on the **seafloor**.

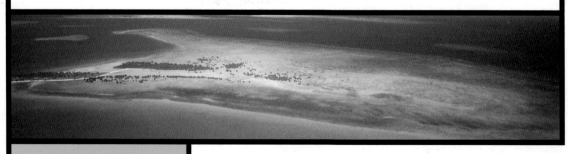

*There are many kinds of coral polyps*

Most coral polyps are smaller than a fingernail. They do not have legs or tails. They cannot move around. They look like little tubes with a mouth. Polyps eat tiny ocean animals.

Many coral polyps look like plants

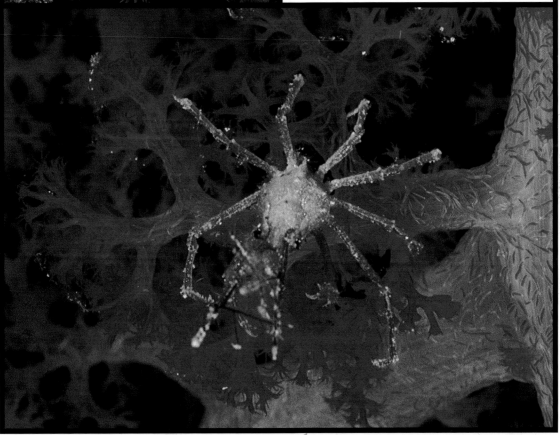

Coral polyps do not have babies. But new polyps grow on the sides of full-grown ones. Lots of polyps grow on top of each other. Big groups of polyps are called colonies *(COL-uh-neez)*.

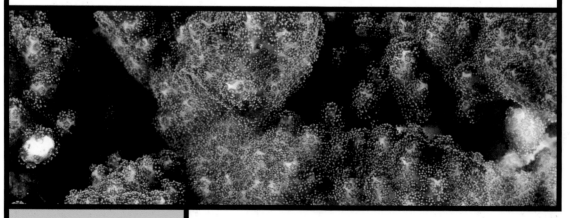

*This coral colony looks like a tree*

*Coral grows in lots
of different shapes*

Different kinds of coral grow in different shapes. Some colonies look like tree branches. Some look like shelves. Some look like feathers. Some even look like brains!

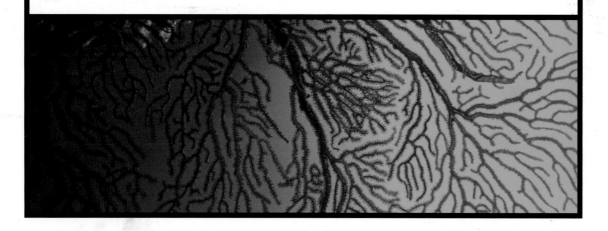

Coral reefs can help make islands

When coral polyps die, their bodies stay in place. They become hard like stone. More polyps grow on top of them. After a long time, the shapes made by the coral polyps get very big. They become a coral reef!

Coral reefs are like houses for lots of animals. Many kinds of colorful fish live in coral reefs. Sharks live there. **Eels** and starfish live there, too. So do crabs and snails.

*Many coral reef
animals are colorful*

Coral reefs have lots of places for animals to hide. There are caves and holes. Animals can hide behind ocean plants, too. All of the colorful animals and plants help make coral reefs bright and pretty.

*Small fish like to hide in coral reefs*

Many people like to visit coral reefs. People go in boats that float over the reefs. They look down into the water. Some people swim in the water to see coral reefs. Coral reefs are like cities in the ocean!

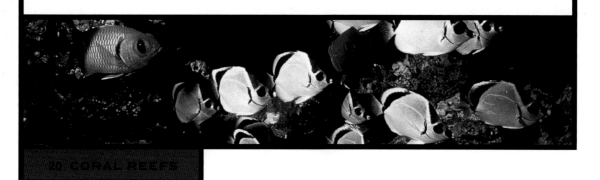

Coral reefs are full of life

The kids' movie *Finding Nemo* is about fish that live in the Great Barrier Reef. Ask your parents or teacher if you can watch it. How many different coral shapes and colors do you see in the movie? How many kinds of fish and animals do you see? Use a pencil and a piece of paper to keep track!

## GLOSSARY

**eels**—skinny fish that look like snakes

**seafloor**—the ground under the water in the ocean

**shallow**—not deep

**structures**—things that are built up by people or animals

## LEARN MORE ABOUT CORAL REEFS

**Enchanted Learning**
http://www.enchantedlearning.com/
biomes/coralreef/coralreef.shtml
*This site has lots of pictures of
coral reef animals.*

**National Marine Sanctuaries**
http://www.hawaiireef.noaa.gov/
education/kids/welcome.html
*This site has coloring pages and
facts about coral reefs.*

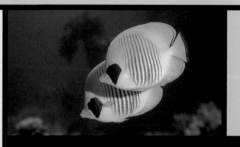

## INDEX